Pink Lotus by Dominique D. Glisson

Published by AfroSoFly Publishing, LLC.
Cover Design: "Lotus Flower Womb" by Chris Anderson
Copyright © 2019 Dominique D. Glisson
All Rights Reserved
ISBN 978-1-7349245-0-3
Ebook ISBN 978-1-7349245-2-7

AfroSoFly.com

No part of this book may be reproduced or transmitted in any form, or by any means, electronic or mechanical, including photocopying, recording or by any information storage or retrieval system without written permission from the publisher.

Sis,

There's no need to go so hard to prove your worth to anyone who is—in fact—not worthy of YOU.

Degradation wears many masks to hide its face. Even though you may be accustomed to pain, you are worthy of love and happiness. You deserve so much more than a man who does not SHOW AND PROVE. We teach men how to treat us by the standards we set and the things we allow.

We have been held captive by men who didn't deserve us for so many years that we are conditioned to starve emotionally in relationships. We are conditioned to chase after love that should already be ours in exchange for our time, bodies, and hearts. We are conditioned to throw reason out of the nearest window just to hold onto any bit of warmth. But are we warm because the sun is shining or are we warm because we are setting ourselves ablaze with our own destructive ways? At some point, we have to realize that we are the only ones with the master key to the locks we've subconsciously placed.

We often want to be THE ONE to make a difference in a man's life when they tell us that all the women they've dated was the same. We enter these toxic situations unsuited—yet ready to endure pain as we try to help wash theirs away—and still come out clean ourselves. However, all we end up with is scars from acid we had no business touching in the first place!

Toxic dick always feels the best but it's a waste of time. The dick be good but all it really does is bring down your value. Toxic is toxic at any level. If you won't take a sip of bleach, keep that same energy when applied to your love life.

Flourish into prosperity of all kinds, Sis! Love yourself as I am learning to love me—FIRST.

Love Always,
Dominique D. Glisson
AfroSoFly ~ Kahawia ~ ButtaFlyy

Table of Contents

Apology to My Womb	Woman
Royally Fucked	Lady
Organ Doning	Queen
Leave It In	Goddess
Lost in Wonderland	Boss
Love Tag	Princess
3 Doors Down	Ma'am
Juicy	Madame
Infinite Growth	Bombshell
26/9	Victress
Acid	Miss
Decay	Heroine
Fed Up	Wife
Ready	Mother
A Thousand Kisses	Auntie
Make it Make Sense	Nana
Home Grown	Sista
Scar	Mami
Inanimate	Female
Bastards	Mom
Lil Sis	Honey
3 AM	Sweetie
Planet Peanut	Superwoman
Hypocrite	Matron

Savage	Babe
Anywhere	Doll
Tails	Amazon
Choices	She
Crack	Cougar
Crayola	Diva
Haiku Series	
Free	Homegirl
Stranger	Homegirl
More & More	Homegirl
Take Dat	Her
Runneth Over	Her
Reset	Her
Pussy	Empress
Vulnerable	Empress
Redemption	Empress
NO!	She
Dominion	She
Turn On	She
Quiet	Beautiful
Drip	Beautiful
Kegels	Beautiful
False Alarm	Warrior
How I Feel	Warrior
She's Lit	Warrior

Apology to My Womb

I've let some monsters climb up
on top of me and into you.
I've knowingly let the undeserving
into your cervix;
into your home;
into your space;
into your feelings—
into your every existence.
I didn't take care of you.
I didn't protect you,
not the way I should have.
I used you
to please myself
and to please another muhfucka
who I knew didn't give a damn.
I've granted niggaz full access
to degrade you;
to rape you—
to fuck you with no conscience.
And I told myself
I was allowing them
to please us both.
I was allowing myself sexual gratification
in exchange for your pain;
in exchange for your tears.
I told myself

that because you allowed me to orgasm,
everything was all good.
I've allowed these two-third ass men
to deflower you.
I used to say that it was to perfection
but your hurt remained unseen.

On several occasions,
I've opened you
to a world
where one could assume
I didn't care about you.
I've even used you for self pleasure
on days when I knew
you didn't feel up to it.
I lusted over my pussy so much
I had very little regard for you.
By some definition of the word,
do you feel assaulted?
How do you feel Beauty?
Cuz to some degree
I do feel as though I've assaulted myself.
I felt how tender you were
when I rubbed on my pussy
to no end—
for my own satisfaction.
I just had to cum
that one more nut
and then

Pink Lotus   *Whats'Her'Name*

two more nuts
and then
'oh shit!'
I haven't fallen asleep yet.
Let me just get one more nut.
I felt you stiffen up
and still
I said, it's alright
just one more.

Look, I got you.
Let me make you feel good,
let me show you
how good you can feel.
I used you.

On more than one occasion,
I used the psychology
that was thrown onto me
onto you.
The psychology that I knew
was bullshit from the jump.
But I convinced myself
that you and I were so good,
it was worth it.
You are a lotus flower
that should've never been plucked
in the first fuckin' place.
After each time,

I would attempt to soothe you
and you'd prick my fingers
with your thorns.
I would tell you
that next time things will be better;
things would be great—
we are doing this for the greater good.
I mean, didn't you feel good just now?
Each time you'd let me know
that no matter how pleasurable
it may have appeared,
I've still sacrificed you.
By allowing worthless negroes
to capture control of my mind
through you.
I used you as a sacrifice
so that I can be a slave
to the dick.
When in all reality,
the shit ain't always been that good.
The best dick
comes from the man who
not only loves you,
but loves me—
loves my heart from his heart.
The best dick
is not pounding us with no regard.

Pink Lotus　　　　　　　　　　　　　　　　　　　　　　　*Skeezer*

From this day on,
I vow to present to you
a strong beautiful brown man
who also vows
to protect you;
to love you;
to feed you life.
You deserve it.
You are worth it.
I will never
lose sight of your worth
again.
I love you.

Royally Fucked

Last night, my man abused his power
Because I was in his possession,
he used me by the hour.
As we lay, my punani is sore
from previous rounds
Yet he is up and ready
like a killer bloodhound
As I wake from my struggle to sleep
with my head pounding like Jack & Jill
on a hill so steep.
I watch as him and his dick play
Then he positions me on the bed
which we lay
He gets the KY and enters from the rear
When I say 'ouch' he acts
as if he doesn't care
As I ride half-heartedly, while I'm on top
With each stroke, I pray he nuts
so we can stop
When I rolled over
and crying was all I could do
He pulled me back
to go round number 2
As he took advantage of my body
in the middle of the night

The room was pitch black
so he could not see me cry
Each moan that escaped my mouth
was pain from him
pounding in and out
I sucked it up and let him continue
because he was horny
I let him further violate my vagina
because he said he loved me
When he finally finished, I faced the wall
for the remainder of the night
And with each attempt,
I removed his arm from my side
One of the craziest things
I've done for love
is allowed myself
to be royally fucked

Organ Doning

The walls are closing in on me
but I'm determined
to recreate space for the wings
given to me to fly far away
from this very place.
The same place
where I was crowned 'silly'
for the men I chose to love
and here I am
realizing that, now
I may only be good enough for a fuck.
Yet, this was the place
I found myself with a cold soul.
I had given up its warmth
to a man who made me feel whole.
Not once, but twice.
I'm gambling with my heart
like it rolls on dice,
$20 for whoever wants it
I'm selling it cheap.
Cuz what good has it done for me,
except giving me the beat
I rely on to breathe?

Leave It In

You wish I could be asleep next to you?
Well, I do too.
In fact, I wish I could fall asleep
with ya dick inside of me.
Right after we collapse from some good lovin'
When you feel yourself rise up from inside
you stroke me 'til we start fuckin'
You caress my breasts
while digging me out
from behind.
In the middle of the night
I hit you with that shimmy you crave all day
and we collide to become one
We sweat and we cum
Then you leave your dick buried deep inside
The nape of my neck meets your lips
for a goodnight kiss.
Holding down the fort 'til you grow again
and again
We sweat and we cum
again.
Mmm...leave it in.

Lost In Wonderland

When an orgasm
makes your internal organs shake
and they feel as if they've lost their place
My brain feels flustered
My kidney wanders like,
"I know I'm supposed
to be somewhere..."
Imagine an orgasm
with more proof than liquor;
one that can subdue my liver
My stomach, all filled
with butterflies and knots
My heart beats undetected.

Pink Lotus   *Princess*

Love Tag

I'm running after a love
that's running from its past
Steady chasing my breath as if it were my last
Many thoughts rummaging through my mind
So much can happen in such little time
I know I'm in love and love conquers all
Strength lands me on my feet
after the greatest fall
So much to be said
but the wrong choice of words
Could lead to someone's feelings being hurt
Back to back holidays; Season's Greeting
In a little over a month,
my love will be leaving
Moving on to chase new dreams
Possibly never coming back for me
Periodic visits replaced
by every once in a blue moon
Due to travel expenses or finding someone new
Life without love can be a living hell
If I'm wrong about the above, keep it to oneself
Change, sometimes, is the ultimate fear
And is often reflected in the salt of my tear

3 Doors Down

Twelve steps down the street
from your childhood home
we sit, to say our goodbyes for the night
Car's parked, in the cut with the lights off
You reach over
to help me with my seatbelt
and realize that you
have not kissed my lips
in a little more than 7 seconds.
8 seconds ago you kissed me
and thought that I would stay
You tongued me down like a knife
plunged into an enemy's jugular
I gasped for air
and as my nipples started to tingle
I put your hands on my breasts
to soothe them as only you could
I placed my hand at the back of your neck
to share the passion I felt
My pussy is wet
and I'm yearning for you…
Yearning for you and your member
while also not wanting a case cuz she ain't
tryna go to jail behind no nut.
So, what do we do?
I reached into the backseat

Pink Lotus   *Hoochie*

>

where I keep an emergency blanket.
Burr! It's fuckin freezing
If I turn on the car,
we'll give away our position
Covered from the waist down
we're both unzipped
My fingers are wrapped around Jr.
to do more
than just keep him warm—
I sang for you,
the most soothing lullaby,
before our goodnight kiss.

Juicy

My honey
gotta have that sweet juice
You know, that slowly
make my heart beat juice
That I wanna see him so bad
I won't go to sleep juice
That when I'm with him,
I'ma miss him when he leave juice
Everybody knows about that
"Thank the Most High I'm finally free" juice
But he gotta have that
"I don't wanna be single,
I want him all for me" juice
That I'll respect his throne
and kiss his feet juice
Okay, maybe not, but it gotta be that alcohol
to prevent infections when I bleed juice
He gotta love to eat
so he can't have that cheap juice
But most of all he gotta be thirsty
for some of Dominique's juice

Infinite Growth

I need to open sesame
and receive your love
I need to receive you
I need for you to feel my legs
tighten on your sides
Bow tied around your back
I need to feel the exclusive intimacy
between penis and womb
I can feel the explosion
of your nut from this angle
I need to feel the weight of our distance
collapse between us
Defeated by the atmosphere of our love
Stroke your shaft
against my walls
I need you to feel
that I feel good
Real good as I nibble on you
however I can
Ever so thankful that you are mine
I ask you how my pussy feels
I need to hear your response
I need you to surf the bottom
Allow me to receive you--all of you
Make me hurt so good

26/9

The burden of monogamy
is weighing heavy on my chest.
Heavier than
having a middle-aged toddler
tugging at my breasts
for affection and all things nutritious.
This union is suffocating,
to say the least
like the pores of a scalp
buried under dandruff
from lack of grease.
I need a good conditioner
We need a third-party in order to survive—
someone who sees you
for more than what meets the eye
or not, but who cares?
I'll settle for just about anyone
willing to split these chores.
I'm thrilled to share time,
conversation, dick,
and anything else that's yours
But not me
I will not share my pussy
between you and someone else
for polygamy is about more
than just myself.

Pink Lotus   *Bird*

Haven't you heard?
There is no such village
with less than six hands
unless that village
has a one-armed man
Yet, even still
There's plenty of you
for another woman to enjoy
leaving me with about 3 or 4 days
to not be annoyed—
to say the very least.

Acid

It's easy to ignore the signs of abuse
Even your heart can put up blinders
and hide the truth
The pattern is there
from the first apology
You know the shit
is bound to go down again
It gets worse
And each outburst
produces harder blows than the last
The thin line between love and trust
will cause you to believe the lie
"it'll never happen again;"
to convince yourself he's playing around
with his threats.
To love him so deeply,
you forget to trust yourself.
The power struggle
is not yours to control.
Any hold he has over you
is toxic to the fruits of your soul.

Decay

Sleepless next to a liar
who sleeps so peacefully
I can't bring myself to snuggle
like the night before
Lying lips all over my body
While the truth hides
beneath the gum line
of your pearly whites
The stench of stray
lingers on your tongue
when you come in from work.

Fed Up

This morning my cousin hit me up
"Yo cuz whatchu doin?"
"Ain't shit chillin"
"Aiight, well come thru and
I'ma take u with me to my shawtii's school"
I'm with it cuz that beats nothing to do
And there she was
5'5" with dark brown, mysterious eyes
I said "what up"
and she barely said "hi"
The 4 of us rode the bus
until it was time to get off
The entire time,
I was listening to how she talked
Although she completely ignored me
I somehow knew
she secretly adored me...

Was I right? Or was I right?
She still brushed me off but my cousin
gave me the number
and I hit her up one night
From his phone tho,
cuz I'm not that brave
Plus she's from Brooklyn
and I didn't wanna get slayed

Pink Lotus   *Jezebel*

We hit it off nice and chilled
over the next few weeks
She told me how her ex was a dick
and she was proud to be free
And so was I, although technically,
I wasn't alone
I spent time with this girl
like I didn't have one at home
I wasn't happy tho'
so it was time for change
and I was sexually frustrated
out of my brain...

So I lied,
when she presented me the sweet deal
of giving me her virginity
I shoulda kept it real
But she knew what it was
I'm sure she could feel
that I was still with my ex
But I took her V
and moved onto the next
She was it!
I told her I loved her
and I pushed that shit
Pussy so good, I wanted her
to have my kids
And I still do...
But I fucked up, ya dig??

I was still fuckin with
the girl before her
I'd be out late at night
and I wouldn't even call her
She never stressed or had titty attacks
So I felt bad and tried to clean up my act
I showed her I loved her
and she did the same
Even when I called her
by someone else's name
She was a rider tho'
she held me down
And I made her cry when I held her down
I violated her body
like some bitch in the streets
Damn, now she won't even look at me...

She was the perfect girl for me
but I let her go
I wanted her to wait for me
while I was out being a ho'
Get this though...
Before I told her to leave
she was already packed
Said she been sick of me
and that she was never coming back
Told me I was a little boy
playing "grown man" all these years

Now I'm sitting in the dark
with one candle lit
crying these grown man tears
Cuz I treated the one woman that cared
like a piece of shit.

Ready

I don't love you as hard as I do
because I'm lonely
I love you so hard
because I'm ready
Ready to love you
in ways that'll show you
I've grown into a woman
capable of loving who you are
Ready to be enthused
about being focused.
Ready to bring forth life and peace
in an effort to soothe chaos.
I love you so hard
because there's no other way
to tend to your heart;
no other way to nourish your soul
than to feed it with the passion
rooted deeply within me
My love, I'm ready.

A Thousand Kisses

When you give your partner head,
it needs to feel
like you're kissing
every part of their body.
The sex thereafter
will be so passionate,
that when it's over
—3 rounds later,
They'll be praising you one minute
and snoring the next.

Make it Make Sense

We talk to the niggaz
who ain't shit
like they are the kings
of all kings.
Then when the king
enters our life,
we act a fuckin' fool!
WHY?

Home Grown

Good love is not found
It's made
And don't be out here
tryna make it with rejects
Fall in love with a man
who loves his mother
Not like "I love her so much—
I can't let her titty go"
But the love that's so good
He has the blueprint
on how to love you
It's a love that feels like home
rather than stuff surrounded by walls.

Scar

If I could peel all my skin
and start over again,
would you love me still
for the scar that I've become?
Would you keep your distance
as I bear the pain of torn flesh
dug into and pulled
by my very own fingertips?
Could you adore me
should my outer layer become a scab?
Would you provide the gauze
for my dripping blood,
or the cocoa butter for me to heal alone?
Could you stand to see me?
Even in my new shield?
Are you as disgusted with me
as I am with myself?

Heads

I need to go to a place
A 5-star hotel, preferably
where I can relax
and enjoy the amenities, alone.
Plush pillows
soft, yet firm mattress
regular ass white sheets
tightly tucked—
The only thing to smother me.
I don't care to socialize
not even on the internets
Room service
Housekeeping
Bartenders
Distanced patrons at the pool—
Limited human interaction.
Let me go
Let me be
I will give you the room key
but DO NOT USE IT!
Unless for an emergency—
dyer.
Wine
a good book
my MacBook
Reruns of my favorite show

Food
and more wine—
This is what solitude looks like.

Inanimate

I am not an inanimate
object that can be picked up
and placed down at anyone's disposal
I cannot be touched,
played with or broken
at the expense of any unsolicited hand
I will not be delicately whispered to
by any old face with a pair of lips
I will not be slipped into someone's pocket
when no one is watching
I will not be bought,
sold, or tossed for donation
I am not without voice,
reason, or defense
I am not without willpower
to not be treated inanimately.

Bastards

Many men who live with women
are under the perception
that SHE
equates to property.
The belief system which allows
them to prey on their target
is one of
corruption
and utter disgust.
There are men
who tell their spouses
that SHE is his to fuck
when/where and howEVER;
that as a wife
SHE has no right to refuse.
Men who tell their women
that SHE must be
fucking the cashier,
the mailman,
the mechanic,
the neighbor,
and anyone else
who dares to wish her "a good day."
Men who tell their women
that they are too plain
to represent him in public;

Pink Lotus   *Chicken Head*

colors too pastel,
name-brand too outdated,
nails unpolished,
—not the trophy he desires.
There are men who
tell their "daughters"
that healthy relationships
may occasionally encounter
sexual assault;
that it's okay,
that it's normal,
that it's to be expected—
to justify their own
acts of sexual assault
against the women
in their lives.
Men who tell their women
that they're not done
after countless rounds
of sweaty sex;
they rip covers,
drag bodies by the legs,
pull closer and rape—
as the pussy that once throbbed
with pleasure
now throbs in pain and bleeds
—while SHE tenses up
and cries.
Who raised these monsters?

Lil Sis

Don't be who I was
before I fully acknowledged
and accepted my worth
Don't be out here dimming your light
for dark niggaz
Always remember,
someone's downfall is not your business
and it damn sure
ain't your responsibility.
Neither is their recovery
If a nigga comes to you
with more issues than *Jet*
leave him the fuck alone.
I'm not saying they don't deserve
chances at love.
I'm saying you need not
make it your business
to prioritize his issues
nor make them yours to solve.
Them niggaz be cute
charming
funny and lovable—
just long enough for you to commit.
Let them niggaz commit
to working on themselves
before allowing them

Pink Lotus   Harlot

                                    to work on you.
                                            Trust.
                                    There are far better
                                 penises that can take you
                                      to higher heights
                                          effortlessly.
                                       Wholesome men
                                   with healthy penises
                                          Good credit.
                                   Men with minimal issues
                             and real plans to work on them.
                                 To be better for themselves,
                                      better suited for you.
                                      Don't be who I was
                             before I truly went after the things
                                       I knew I deserved
                             Use what you've seen and combine it
                                     with what you've heard
                                  To be the best version of you
                             as you were destined since birth.

3 A.M.

Prying through his hold
in the middle of the night
Just so I could pee
I'd almost rather keep a full bladder
Under his arm
feels like a sauna
My nose is stuffed to capacity
I can only breathe,
for real, through my mouth
Even though I must relieve my urethra
and I'm as hot as two fucks
on a summer day
I'm grateful for this
compromising position
My King's embrace is so secure.

Planet Peanut

Sometimes new situations
have a tendency to feel
like a breath of fresh air.
But THIS union
is like a whole
new
planet!
Deep waters.
Clean air
and vegetation.
Gardens from edge to edge
filled with pure alkalinity.
Sweet sounds
of happy children learning
and sharing.

Hypocrite

I've supported women by telling them,
"There's no reason a man
should ever hit a woman."
I also intend to teach my sons
that under NO circumstance
should a woman raise her hand to them as well.
Yet, I laid hands on you.
I found multiple reasons to strike you
on several occasions.
Every disrespectful word that left your mouth
landed a jab to your chest.
Careful not to scar your face
and raise questions.
Shoulder hits,
right hooks to your arms.
I charged at you with dishes and beer bottles.
Every false accusation resting upon your lips
landed a reverse to the wall
closest to your nose.
I've had nightmares
of bashing your skull in the worst way.
I've thought of plenty of reasons
why you deserve such a tragic ending.
After all,
you provoked me;
you spoke out of turn

Pink Lotus *Sex Kitten*

from the side of your neck;
you attacked my character
with your words;
you were next-level disrespectful
on many occasions;
and the list goes on.
We traded stories
of who would end who first.
—You tried it.

<u>Savage</u>

A nigga will ask
if he's the best you've ever had;
if his dick is bigger than ya last;
if his tongue gets you wetter than baths?
A nigga will beg and plead
for you to lie to his face;
for you to say anything to make his day;
for you to make him believe
he's the icing on ya cake.
A nigga will swear
that he wanna know the truth;
that he wants to know the real you;
that he won't be heartbroken when you do.
Bet!
You used to be the best
before I learned better.
I've been with niggaz
that had my pussy way wetter.
Ya dick game's legit,
glad that you're a grower,
but my pussy's a vet
so ain't much you can show her.
I never fucked ya friends,
despite what you think.
Sometimes I struggled to fuck you,
that's why I would drink.

Pink Lotus *Pigeon*

You wasn't all bad,
you had good shit about you.
But doubting yourself,
gave me plenty reason to doubt you.
You ain't never been a nigga
for me to be with.
Point blank
PeriodT!

Anywhere

I feel like I have a tampon
where your dick should be
All puns intended.
As I wait for my monthly visitor to leave,
I reminisce...
Your dick was in my vagina so deep,
I can taste it on my tongue—
Mouth open wide, thirsting to be
stuffed in ways unimaginable.
I often have visions
of being dug out deeply
from behind,
in the midst of awkward spaces:
grocery lines
traffic lights
conversations
funerals
waiting rooms
board meetings
crossing bridges
physical therapy
break rooms
—You name it.

Tails

Snuggle next to me
at night and in the morning
Leaving space between us
in the middle
Still desiring to know you're near
my leg shall rest upon yours
Laid back
my head neatly tucked
under your arm
Comfortably—
Sneak up behind me in the kitchen
Plant kisses on my flower
Tell me you miss me
since I've gotten out of bed
Twirl me around
dance with me
pull me close
secure
embrace
constant contact
These moments
I cherish and adore the most.

Choices

Just because you choose
to go to a nigga crib
at two in the morning
after you're done with school
done with work
done with your day
to get laid, doesn't mean
you don't respect yourself.
Maybe you don't respect
that nigga enough
to give him more of YOU.
Why you gotta be out here
searching for
a nigga to give you all of him?
Just cuz he got good dick
don't mean he has good mannerisms
or that he's a good dude.
Having good dick doesn't qualify
him for shit, on a love scale.
Let's be honest.
I'm not saying that
'all dudes with good dick
are horrible'
but 6 times out of 10
they ain't shit.
All they got is dick.

So why not come through
get what he got
and be out?
Now, I understand
that energies exchange.
People with good dick
and good pussy
can have fucked up energies.
However,
that's why we have sage
and yoni pearls
that's why we detox our bodies
detox our minds
detox our spirits
detox our lives.
you can still make the best
of getting laid.
You don't gotta fuck the nigga
every night.
Once or twice a week
maybe just 3 nights the first week,
then don't see him again
for about 2 months.
If that's what you choose
consciously
it doesn't mean you lack self respect.
Stop letting society tell you
that you're supposed to grow up
to find a husband

and nothing else.
Sis,
hop on and ride
as many ponies as you choose
until you feel satisfied.
How about that?
Even if you only hop on 3 ponies.
Ride them until there's no more
—if you choose to.
We always have choices.
Respect yourself within your choices
and you'll be aiight.
Love yourself within your choices
and you'll
be
aiight.

Crack

Babies birthed
under harsh circumstances
Left behind
brought up in loneliness
Surrounded by humans
who love differently
Humans who love drugs
more than they love kin
Humans who reconstruct bones
with the use of their fists
Humans who only come around
for pagan feasts
Humans who've been molesting children
since way back when
Humans who equate
material possessions
with affection
Humans who use fear
as a means to an end
Humans who use the system
for a welfare check—
false DV accusations
overly "diagnosing" the youth
Humans who place babies
in prison with grown men

Humans who build liquor stores
rather than shelters
Humans who deny
symptoms of deficiency
Humans who kill
to let out frustration
Humans who may not
really be humans at all—
Reptilians that shoot
hang and drag
just for sport
Reptilians that colonize
for monetary gain
Reptilians that capitalize
on creating broken homes
Reptilians that purchase souls
for pennies on a dollar—
Black don't crack on the outside
cuz it's too busy shattering internally.

Crayola

Color me stupid
for being a friend
Color me blind
for not seeing it then
Color me hurt
for coloring a man
The same man
who colored me pain again
Color me smart
for making it out of high school
Color me homeless
for I am limited to where I can move
Color me sex
since he loves it so much
Color me unsatisfied
after each time we fuck
Color me roses
for blooming with pride
Color me deaf
for not hearing the little voice inside
Color me shit
for hanging with assholes
Color me single
cuz at times I'd rather be alone
Color me faithful
for I would never be tempted to cheat

Color me success
cuz I've experienced defeat
Color me sleep,
my body deserves the rest
Color me sore,
my punani deserves the sex
Color me stupid
again, but use a different term
Color me a heart,
not broken but burned
Color me simple
for not thinking with my head
And just for it being my favorite,
color me red.

Haiku Series

Free

You tried to kill me
and I've been free ever since.
I'm no longer yours.

Stranger

I never knew you
You just happened to be there
I do not love you.

More & More

Orgasms are not
all there is to sex. But I
prefer to have four.

Take Dat

To relieve myself
I pop my pussy real quick,
before you return.

Runneth Over

I masturbated
17 times in one day.
I felt so damn good.

Reset

I have wasted words,
time, space, and energy too.
Control, Alt, Delete.

Pussy

Pussies are pussies
Fuck them into submission
Listen to them purr.

Vulnerable

It's not wrong to need
or be needed in return—
My love, I need you.

Redemption

I have un-fucked you
and all the others, as well.
I'm a new virgin.

NO!

Fuck boys are at large
approaching from all angles.
Leave them where they stand.

Dominion

My right side is right.
My left side's mostly heartfelt.
I rest in between.
(inspired by She who mothers many)

Turn On

He loves my shimmy.
Each time we lay, shit gets real.
Just enough wiggle.

Quiet!

Snoring is not cute.
Don't be up under me with
all that gotdamn noise!
(a message from the Sleepless Wives Club)

Drip

My coochie glitters
This drip drips like no other
Cum get bedazzled.

Kegels

Squeeze, release...repeat
all day long, tighten your cooch
#NoLooseWalls

False Alarm

I thought I loved you
but then I saw your penis.
Too small, love gone...bye!

How I Feel

How can you lead me
if you're always asking me
"Where do we go now?"

She's Lit

She is poetry.
Her tongue spoke this language first.
Poetry is She.

I take ownership for all of my failed relationships because for every man I allowed to violate me, I did it to myself. Since I didn't make the change to do away with them after the first violation, the rest is ultimately on me. Ownership makes me accountable for my future.

Pink Canvas was my first step of acknowledgment. I have come to terms with my flaws, my likes, my woes, my feelings—and that of my womb.

Thank you for taking this journey with me as I travel through life searching for self whilst associating with men I've chosen to fuck, love, and whatever else.

Link me...

IG: Kahawia__
Kahawia.com

Stay tuned for the final part of the Pink Trilogy.

www.ingramcontent.com/pod-product-compliance
Lightning Source LLC
Chambersburg PA
CBHW021123080526
44587CB00010B/619